Symbols of faith – conveying meaning

Symbolism is the language of religion. Symbols, whether they be objects, actions, sounds or language, are open to interpretation at many levels – they draw out multi-layered responses, memories and associations. Symbols disclose. Unlike 'signs', which are clear, unambiguous statements, symbols contain a multiplicity of meaning. They demand that we work them out, that we reflect, ponder, ask questions and make connections.

Encouraging pupils to look for the meaning in an artefact, a religious story, a picture, or a religious sound, action, gesture or object is central to good learning in RE. RE should help pupils to 'see', to look for 'more than meets the eye', to delve beneath the surface, to ask questions about deeper meaning and purpose. Good teachers recognise this and give pupils the time and the structures to enable them to explore, ask questions, reflect, and express their own ideas about meaning.

This publication aims to help you with some strategies and ideas to help pupils develop and use these skills in your classroom. Together you will be able to listen to sounds, explore images and pictures, make up metaphors, develop movements and express ideas through dance and drama. Such multi-sensory and active strategies will appeal to a wide range of different learning needs and help pupils of a wide range of abilities achieve well and enjoy their RE.

Joyce Mackley
Editor

Contents

Looking for meaning
Some approaches to learning in RE

Enabling pupils to look for the meaning of actions, artefacts, objects, stories and pictures used in religion, and then encouraging pupils to have the confidence and skills to express their own ideas about these, is at the heart of RE.

Helping pupils to interpret meaning

Pupils with the ability to 'interpret' in RE are able to 'draw meaning' from artefacts, literature, art, religious gesture and symbolism.

Given the right opportunities, children from the early years can suggest what religious stories, pictures, actions and objects say or mean.

Ask a 6-year-old to pick out a 'holy person' in a nativity scene – they will show you the one with the halo. Ask an 8-year-old to suggest why a Hindu might ring a bell during worship – lots of thoughtful and appropriate ideas follow. Ask a 10-year-old to work out a movement or dance to show how the Jews might have felt at the time of the Passover – and all the joy and excitement of freedom is expressed.

See also...

The activities opposite fit well with QCA scheme of work 3A: What do signs and symbols mean in religion?

Some useful websites

- Simple instructions for making a gragger:
  www.blewa.co.uk/project4/teachers/T4–2–4–2.htm
- Songs for Jewish festivals:
  www.twocandles.com

Some planning steps for teachers

- **Be clear** about what it is you want pupils to interpret. Identify the meaning or significance for yourself first, Look for links with pupils own experience and plan activities to build on these.

- **Set the right tasks** (e.g. a feely bag activity to engage younger children with the object; a paired activity for older pupils to give first responses to a picture; an object, a video clip; an artefact; movement and art activities to express a key moment in a story).

- **Ask probing open questions** (e.g. What do you think this means? How might a believer use this?)

- **Give pupils the time** to reflect and express their own ideas. Avoid the temptation to 'provide the answers'.

What sort of tasks work best?

We all learn best in different ways. Some prefer to look and observe (**visual** tasks), others prefer to listen (**auditory** tasks) and many enjoy activities which use movement (**kinaesthetic**). VAK is a useful planning tool to ensure a range of activities. On the next page we've listed some ways of introducing symbolic actions and objects to younger children under these headings. You will be able to add your own ideas.

- Dreidel game details:
  www.akhlah.com/holidays/hanukkah/Dreidel.asp
  www.holidays.net/chanukah/pattern.html

Introducing symbolic actions and objects

Visual: What can we look at?

Pictures, posters and photographs of religious people, worship and festivals; artwork and religious pictures such as icons. Ask: What do you see? How does it make you feel? What do you want to ask? How is the person feeling? How do you know? What do the colours and shapes tell you?

Artefacts: symbols (e.g. cross); books (e.g. Qur'an or Torah scrolls); costume (e.g. clerical 'dog' collar or ihram worn by Muslims on pilgrimage); food (e.g. challah bread at Shabbat or Easter eggs); greetings cards (e.g. Eid or baptismal); other (e.g. Advent calendars).

Video or website images: Schools broadcasts, e.g. the BBC *Watch* series, show real lives and animated faith stories. Use carefully selected clips of secular stories (e.g. *The Snowman*) to focus on a feeling or experience relevant to the RE focus. Using the video, freeze-frame a moment and ask questions such as: What is he or she thinking or feeling? What do you think happens next?

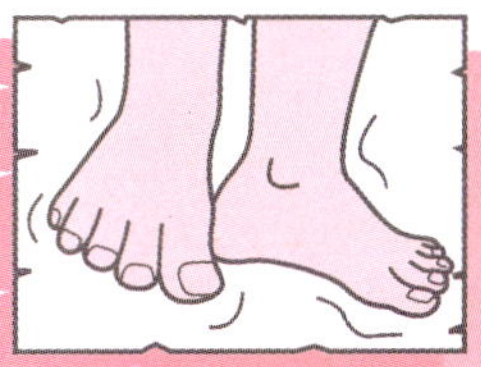

Kinaesthetic: Let's get moving!

Role-play

Dressing-up box for very young children: this extends children's experiences, e.g. multicultural saris or shalwar kameez. Appropriate when exploring Hindu and Muslim stories and festivals, but avoid dressing up in explicitly religious items (see page 26).

Acting out

- **Modelling respect:** Make a shoe rack using stacked shoeboxes. Younger pupils could 'act out' how Muslims and Sikhs remove their shoes when entering the mosque or gurdwara.

- **Practising actions** which convey meaning, e.g. Namaste (hands together) – 'peace be with you'.

Auditory: What can we listen to?

Story activities

Work out sounds pupils can make whenever certain names or words are used during the telling of a faith story. This is fun and a great way of keeping their attention. For example: stamping feet like soldiers marching as the Pharaoh's soldiers hunt for baby Moses; making a loud noise (traditionally the shaking of a gragger) at the mention of Haman in the telling of the story of Esther (Jewish spring festival of Purim).

Sounds

Listen to sound files from faith traditions, such as the adhan (call to prayer) in Islam and talk about how they are used and how they make you feel.

Music and singing

- **Sing children's songs for religious festivals,** such as Christian stories told through action songs; the Christmas story put to music children know; Jewish Hanukkah songs.

- **Connect music to feelings** (linked to worship), e.g. happy music for celebrating special times like a wedding and for saying thank you.

- **Use music to aid reflection**, e.g. as they write or draw their response to a faith story or teaching.

- **Expressing feelings** – link with how people worship (arms raised – joy; head bowed – respect or reflection; etc.) Links to Hindu, Jewish or Christian dance and music.

- **Recreating faith group activities**, e.g. building a wooden-framed sukkot in the school hall as part of a harvest theme to recreate how Jews build huts outside and eat or sometimes sleep there as part of their Jewish autumn harvest festival.

Play a game

Hanukkah: try playing the dreidel game, in which the four-sided dreidel is spun. Traditionally the game is played as the candles burn down (about 30 minutes).

Introducing symbolic actions, gestures and images

Activities for younger primary pupils

For the teacher

Teaching activities which will provide a foundation for younger pupils to build on will enable children to....

- **experience symbolic actions or gestures**, including rituals which form part of a ceremony (such as in an infant baptism) and be able to talk about the feelings these show;

- **use their senses** (as appropriate) to explore the special nature, meaning and value of artefacts for religious believers;

- **listen to and talk about a variety of sounds and imagery** used in worship and celebrations.

Activity for pupils: Worship at home (for 6–7-year-olds)

- Introduce objects which 'represent' aspects of family life and use them to talk about the sorts of things families do together e.g. cutlery (eat together); football or boardgame (play together); bucket and spade (go on holiday); birthday card (celebrate special days); plastic carrier bag (go shopping together); book (read together). Children could suggest or draw some of their own 'symbols' for things they do in their families.

- Introduce some artefacts associated with particular faith homes:
  - Bible; rosary beads; cross; prayer book (Christian).
  - Qur'an; prayer mat; compass; headscarf or cap (Muslim).
  - Mezuzah; Sabbath candles; kippah (Jewish).
  - Puja set (Hindu).
  - Pictures of Guru Nanak (Sikh).

Using mime, role-play, story, video clips and/or feely bag activities, enable children to talk about what they are, how they are used and why they are important to believers.

Activity for pupils: Saying 'Thank you' (for 5–6-year-olds)

- How do you show you are pleased?

- How do Christians say thank you to God? (Praise, Lord's Prayer, harvest festival.)

- How do Christians and Jews say thank you to God for the beautiful world we live in? (Harvest festival or Sukkoth link.)

- Listen to a poem such as 'All we need' by Steve Turner (Lion, ISBN 0-7459-3640-7). Talk about things we need but sometimes forget to say thank you for (e.g. food, friends, homes, sunshine, rain), and make a display.

- Talk about how children can express thanks for the things they are grateful for – what could they say and do to convey this inner feeling to others? Mime gestures of thanks and love.

- Children could make thank you cards to special people or to God or write a simple prayer or poem called 'Thank you' expressing thanks for their favourite things. Share these with the class.

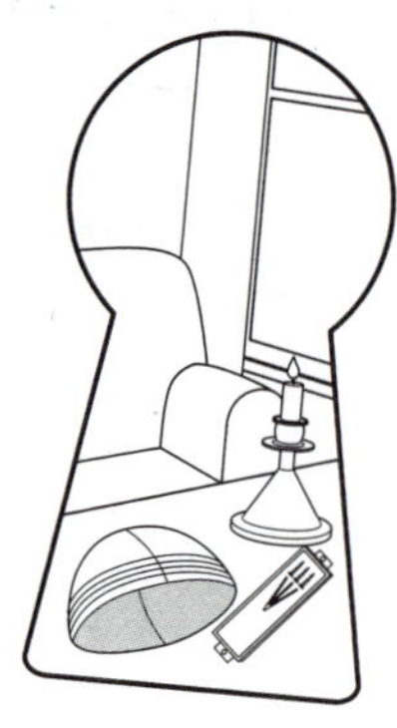

Activities for older primary pupils

For the teacher

Teaching activities should provide older pupils with opportunities to:

- **explore** the symbolic use of a wide range of objects, sounds, visual images, actions and gestures;
- **make observations** as to the intended meaning they have for believers.

Activity for pupils
(for 10–11-year-olds)

Christians have many symbols to show what is important to them. Some come from the time when it was dangerous to be a Christian and secret signs had to be used.

Look carefully at these eight symbols. They each say something important about God. What do you think is their hidden meaning?

a God knows everything, sees everything.

b God is always present.

c God cares for people.

d God frees people to live their lives fully

e God knows what it is like to suffer.

f People can put their trust in God.

g God sends his peace and help to those who trust him.

Activity for pupils:
Expressing important ideas
(for 8–9-year-olds)

→ Choose a key idea or value such as **love**, **peace** or **justice**.

→ Ask pupils to talk about why this is important. What would the world, this village or town, or this school be like without it?

→ Ask children if we can see it. Talk about abstract ideas – things we can't see, which don't have a shape, but which affect us all. Can children suggest any others?

→ Talk about the school badge or symbol – if you have one. What 'important ideas' is this expressing? Can pupils design a symbol or visual image to express the 'important idea' they have chosen (love, peace, etc..)?

→ Explore what Christianity teaches about the idea – love, peace, justice. Ask pupils to add further symbols to theirs to include some of these Christian ideas.

A summative creative activity

Design, using a range of Christian symbols, one of the following. Write a brief report explaining the features of your design and why you chose them.

- A stained glass window.
- A banner or wall hanging for a school assembly hall.
- A badge for a new church school.

Exploring actions and gestures used in worship

The following pages provide some suggestions for exploring how actions and gestures are used in worship to convey meaning. Activities focus on prayer and dance, and specifically relate to Christianity, Islam and Hinduism. They may be adapted to other religions.

For the teacher

Religious traditions use a range of actions and gestures to express inner feelings and beliefs in worship.

Some examples from Christian worship

Hands: raised in praise; clapping in rhythm; hands together or palms uppermost in prayer; making the sign of the cross (e.g. on a baby's head at baptism); crossing oneself; holding hands during communal prayer; laying on of hands to pray over or to heal someone; sharing the peace by shaking hands; holding a Bible when making a vow; breaking bread and elevating the host.

Bodies: standing or kneeling for prayer; head bowed; swaying or dancing to worship songs; processing in church with a cross; lighting a candle for prayer.

Examples from Hindu worship

Hands: Using prayer beads; performing the arti ceremony and receiving the flame; ringing a bell and offering food during puja; making namaste – the traditional hands-together gesture of Hindu greeting for friends and colleagues and used to pay respect to an elder, a holy person or to a deity.

Bodies: removing shoes for prayer; standing and bowing for worship.

Examples from Muslim worship

Hands: Using prayer beads (subha).

Bodies: removing shoes for prayer; washing before prayer (performing wudu); standing in rows for prayer; moving through prayer positions (rak'ahs).

Heads: covering the head for prayer; facing Makkah for prayer.

Expectations

It is important to be clear about what you want pupils to know, understand and be able to do by the end of the teaching activity. Below you will see three 'I can' statements which describe such outcomes in a pupil-friendly way. These are based on the QCA expectations for most 7-year-olds in RE (level 2), and 11-year-olds (level 4) matched to the content of the teaching unit.

I can talk about what I think some movements in a Hindu dance might mean and mime some things people do to show how they feel inside.
(level 1)

I can mime some actions which show friendship, thanks and kindness to others and describe some things religious people do to show that they think God is very important.
(level 2)

I can describe and explain some symbolic movements used by Muslims and Hindus when they worship, use movement to express my own understanding of the meaning of a faith story and draw informed and thoughtful conclusions about the importance of prayer for Muslims from what some Muslims say.
(Level 4)

Things to note

The curriculum ideas in this section complement QCA schemes of work:

4a How and why do Hindus worship at home and in the mandir?

5b How do Muslims express their beliefs through practices?

6f How do people express their faith through the arts?

Activities for lower primary pupils: Exploring Hindu story through dance

For the teacher

A traditional way of communicating religious stories in Hinduism is through dance. Hindu dance uses eye, hand and arm movements to symbolise the key events in the story. Try working out a few simple movements for pupils to mime as a starting point. This is a good way of getting children to really think about the story and, at the same time, develop their non-verbal communication skills! Lower primary pupils enjoy this sort of activity – but it is easily adaptable for use with upper primary pupils as well.

Getting started

- Tell a simple version of a traditional Hindu faith story. Tales might include:
  - one of the stories of Krishna, such as his birth, thieving butter, stars in his mouth, dancing on the serpent Kaliya's head or dancing with the cow-girls;
  - a story about Ganesha, such as how he got his elephant head or the story of his belly bursting.
- Explain to children that these stories are often 'told' by dancers. Talk about how they might do this.
- Ideally, invite a Hindu dancer into school to show pupils some actions and gestures. If this isn't possible, show a video clip of a Hindu dance.
- Notice carefully the movements. If using a video, freeze-frame and ask children to copy the position.
- Talk about what it might be 'saying' – what do they think it means?
- After watching the video and when pupils are more confident, try creating together a dance based on a Hindu creation story.

Developing a 'creation' dance

- Pupils listen to traditional Hindu music and try out gestures for different animals (e.g. birds, monkeys, elephants) moving in different ways (quickly, grumpily, slyly) to the music. They could practise these using their whole bodies then try using different parts of their bodies, such as hands and arms, heads and eyes, and legs and feet. Pupils could also try out their own different free movements to the music.
- Divide the story into sections, giving pupils in threes a small section of the story to work on. Choosing key characters and moments in the story, groups explore hand, arm, head, eye, leg or foot movements to depict the character or moment in the story. These can be practised and performed to the rest of the class.
- The entire story can be re-told through dance with each group performing their section in turn.

The cross-curricular and multicultural aspects of this could be further developed by making masks and wearing costumes and saris, using traditional Indian fabrics.

See also....

- *Quest Creation Stories: Hinduism* (Channel 4 Schools, ISBN 1-899214-91-7) and *Teachers' Guide* (Channel 4 Schools, ISBN 1-899214-330-X). www.channel4.com/learning/shop A Hindu creation story is retold through dance. A dancer explains some of the hand gestures to children.
- *Developing Primary RE: Special Places* (RE Today Services). Includes three Hindu creation stories.
- *A to Z: Practical learning strategies* (RE Today Services). Contains more details about using dance in RE.

Activities for upper primary pupils: Exploring dance in Christian worship

For the teacher

Christians of various traditions have taken the words of psalms, hymns and songs and expressed their meaning and beliefs through dance. Dance is a means of expressing a range of emotions and experiences. Asking pupils to reinterpret music and words into movement is a good activity to promote the important RE skills of reflection, interpretation and the expression of meaning.

Activities for pupils

→ Use recordings of Christian songs or hymns – or select songs pupils know well from collective worship and record them for RE. The initial focus might be on songs expressing praise to God.

→ Give pupils copies of the words and listen to the recording. Pupils work with a partner to consider the meaning of the words. Ask them to underline any words they are unsure about. These could be looked up in the dictionary before discussion with the whole class.

→ Read through the words of the song with the class, using the words as a guided visualisation, asking pupils to close their eyes and consider what they see in their mind's eye when they hear the words being read. What do they feel? How might they show how they feel?

→ Pupils work in pairs to plan a movement to a verse they choose. Give them opportunities during the planning to listen to the song again as they rehearse.

→ Different verses can be performed to the rest of the class or to other classes, or used in class assemblies. Digital or video cameras could be used to record performances.

→ Pupils might later create music for Christian prayers, then prepare a dance or mime to go with them. Examples include the Lord's Prayer, the grace, the prayer of Saint Francis, the Hail Mary and the Gloria.

→ Give pupils the opportunity to express how they felt when participating in the songs. Can they suggest how the songs might make a Christian feel?

A Christian song which could be choreographed is 'Lord of the Dance':

I danced in the morning
When the world was begun
And I danced in the moon
And the stars and the sun
And I came down from heaven
And I danced on the earth –
At Bethlehem I had my birth.

Dance, then, wherever you may be,
I am the Lord of the Dance, said he,
And I'll lead you all, wherever you may be
And I'll lead you all in the dance, said he.

I danced for the scribe
And the Pharisee
But they would not dance
And they wouldn't follow me,
I danced for the fishermen
For James and John –
They came with me
And the dance went on.

I danced on the Sabbath
And I cured the lame
The holy people
Said it was a shame
They whipped and they stripped
And they hung me high
And they left me there
On a cross to die.

I danced on a Friday
When the sky turned black –
It's hard to dance
With the devil on your back
They buried my body
And they thought I'd gone
But I am the dance
And I still go on.

They cut me down
And I leapt up high –
I am the life
That'll never, never die
I'll live in you
If you'll live in me
I am the Lord
Of the Dance, said he.

By Sydney Carter (1915–2004), © Stainer & Bell Ltd, reproduced by permission.

Activities for upper primary pupils:
Prayer in Islam

For the teacher

When Muslims pray, it is with their bodies as well as with words. The traditional set of movements known as rak'at is made up of recitation, standing, bowing and two prostrations.

The following activities are designed to encourage pupils to reflect on the meaning of these movements and to consider the significance of   prayer for Muslim children. The quotations on page 10 are from the *Children Talking* website: www.pcfre.org.uk/db

Activity for pupils 1:
Exploring how Muslims pray

→ Watch a video clip showing Muslims performing salah, with the sound down. Ask pupils to look carefully at the prayer movements. The Muslim website www.jannah.com/learn/flashprayer1.html contains a useful downloadable presentation called 'Prophet Muhammad's manner of doing prayers'.

→ Whilst watching the rak'ah, ask pupils to make sketches of as many different prayer positions as they can pick out.

→ For each position, ask pupils to annotate the sketch to explain what they think the movement might mean or say about the worshippers' inner feelings and beliefs.

→ Watch the clip again with the sound up. Notice what is said about the meaning of each movement. Compare with pupils' own ideas.

→ Invite a Muslim into class to show the rak'ahs (prayer positions) and talk about and answer questions about what prayer means to them.

→ Pupils design a poster illustrating one of the rak'ahs, ensuring that all positions are selected throughout the class. Alongside the drawing of the position, pupils add a 'thought bubble' suggesting what they think a Muslim might be thinking when they are in this position before Allah. Alongside the illustration, pupils write down what they think the gesture in the rak'ah might mean. Display pupils' work in the correct order of the rak'ahs.

Activity for pupils 2:
Exploring the significance of prayer for Muslims

→ Explain the aim of the activity to pupils. In mixed ability groups of three, they are to read through and sort out quotes from Muslim pupils to help them answer the question, 'Why is prayer so important for Muslims?

→ Give pupils a pack of quotes copied and cut out from page 10.

• Ask pupils to prioritise the statements into a diamond shape according to how helpful they are in explaining why prayer is so important to Muslims, putting the most helpful at the top, least helpful at the bottom.

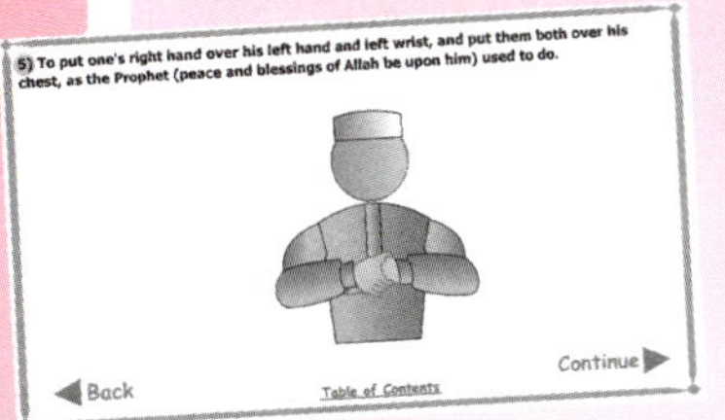

• Each person in the group chooses one of the statements and answers the following:
• Why did you choose this statement? What interests you about it?

• What is being said, and what does it mean? What does the person believe and why do you think they believe this?

→ Pupils produce a statement of not more than thirty words to answer the question 'Why is prayer so important for Muslims?' If possible, ask a local Muslim to read and respond to the pupils' statements.

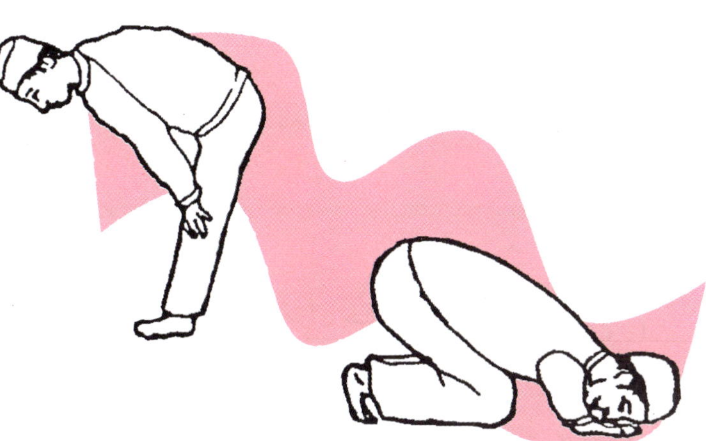

What Muslim pupils say about prayer

When you pray, you feel closer to God.
You thank him for what you have got.

In Islam by praying five times a day
we get the reward and get to know
our religion better.

Daily prayers are important
because when we worship God
we are talking to Allah.

Prayer makes me feel more lively
and responsible. It makes me feel
strong in my faith.

It is very difficult to describe exactly
how prayer makes me feel. One feeling is
being refreshed, and ready to carry on
with the rest of the day.

Prayers are important because
you are thanking God for
what you have and for giving you life.

Prayer makes me feel that
I am communicating with God.
It should help us stop doing evil.

When I pray, I feel very relaxed and
happy, especially on the Friday Prayer,
which keeps us Muslims together.

The more a person prays,
the stronger his or her beliefs become.
The stronger the belief in a religion
(which teaches the way of life),
the better a person will become.

Praying is something solemn, not a joke.
It should make us feel close to Allah,
just as if He is right there
in front of us.

I think prayer is the most important
way of showing your love to Allah.
I think that the important thing
is what's in your heart and
how you live your life for Allah.

Prayer makes me feel like
a new person inside.

If you begin with the name of Allah,
then Allah will help you.

I think prayer is when you talk to Allah
about things or ask for forgiveness,
help and give thanks. The more you get
to know someone the more they get to
know you and it is the same with Allah.

When you pray, you feel comfort
and peace. You feel closer to Allah.

Using sounds and music to help pupils learn in RE

For the teacher

Sound – and the absence of sound – is a powerful medium through which religion is experienced, expressed and communicated: singing, music, saying prayers, chanting, performing a liturgy, ringing bells, and more … all have their part to play in many religious traditions.

Engaging pupils with these sounds can be done in a variety of ways which are consistent with the demands of RE syllabuses, and which also draw upon and complement other aspects of the curriculum, such as music.

The activities suggested here focus on Christianity and Sikhism, yet can be readily adapted to support work on other faiths.

Sun Sounds

If we could hear the sun
would it buzz
like a nest of giant bees?
Would it twitter
like a treeful of birds?
Would it fizz
like a streetful of frying pans?
Would it boom
like a skyful of fireworks?
Or
would it roar
like a worldful of ovens?

From Centrally Heated Knickers *by Michael Rosen (Puffin, 2000, ISBN 0-14-130671-8)*

Activities for pupils: three ideas to get you started

The following activities suggest some ways of getting pupils to be open and responsive to the sounds around them; to get them to be more able to 'listen with awareness' and to begin to think about the how religious faiths often use sounds to express very deep and important things.

A stilling activity which literally 'stills' or calms the body and mind is a helpful start to the lesson. (See *A to Z: Practical learning strategies* from RE Today Services.)

- **Focus on the words** of the poem 'Sun Sounds'. Ask pupils to respond actively to the sounds described, making the sounds in different styles, e.g. buzz like a nest of 'angry bees' and then 'contented bees'. Pupils compose their own poems, e.g. 'Garden sounds'.

- **Go on a 'listening walk'** and note all the sounds you hear. If it's not possible to go outside, open a window, ask pupils to hold both fists in the air, eyes closed. Every time someone hears a different sound they lift a finger. **Talk about**: Who has the best hearing? What did they hear? How do they feel when there is no sound at all? What sounds make us happy, sad, or excited?

- **Focus on the experience** described in 'The sounds of sand dunes'. Ask pupils to focus on the feelings as well as the sounds. Provide opportunities for them to draw the noise that sand dunes make, or to draw what the word silence 'looks like'.

The sounds of sand dunes

Climbing to the crest of a desert sand dune, I heard:

'You simply must slide down and push off.'

Following my host's advice, I tobogganed from the dune's curving peak. Beneath me, a million sand grains shifted and slid. And the most extraordinary thing happened. The whole dune began to hum and resonate, its bowl making a deep roaring sound.

The movement of the sand grains had generated vibrations that were amplified by the natural loudspeaker shape of the dune and my slide had become a deafening experience.'

© John Stringer, a teacher of primary science in the Middle East. Reproduced from the Times Educational Supplement *by kind permission of the author.*

Using sound to support learning in RE – some tips for teachers

The following general guidelines will help you get the most out of activities using sounds and listening:

→ A **stilling activity** can help create an appropriate atmosphere for work using sound. A stilling activity usually involves:

- relaxation – sitting alert with hands resting on lap. Listening to sounds outside the room, inside the room and finally focusing attention on one's own breathing.
- attentive listening – often taking part in a guided visualisation with the teacher taking the pupils on an imaginary journey which includes sensory experiences, through the asking of questions such as 'What do you hear? What can you smell? What can you "see"? What do you want to ask or say?'
- a follow-up opportunity to express personal ideas and insights (often in a creative way) and the sharing of ideas and experiences (with no obligation to join in).

→ **Encourage children to be quiet** both before and after the sound is played or performed.

→ Allow time and provide a structure for pupils to 'interpret' the music – 'What does it say? What is the composer telling us? How does it make you feel?'

→ **Design a listening frame** to encourage active and well-focused listening. See the 'Ways to Listen' section of the Primary National Strategy 'Listening – making it work in the classroom' poster (published 2003).

→ **Provide opportunity for a variety of responses** to the sound(s) used, e.g.

- movement or dance (respond to the sound; create own dance to express understanding of the theme);
- artwork (a visual expression of the theme expressed in the music, e.g. forgiveness, hope, joy);
- making sounds during the telling of a faith story (e.g. marching army in the story of David and Goliath);
- writing (e.g. writing another verse to a worship song).

The following two pages offer some practical approaches to teaching Christianity and Sikhism, making effective use of sound and music. As with all planning, it is important to be clear about what you want pupils to know, understand and be able to do by the end of the teaching activity. It is helpful to express your expectations in pupil-friendly language. The 'I can...' statements below are some examples.

Expectations – Christianity activities

The following statements are based on the non-statutory QCA expectations for most 6-year-olds in RE, matched to the activities suggested on page 13.

- I can make some music and sounds which help to tell a story from the Bible. *(Level 1)*
- I can say how the music and sounds used in religion make me feel. *(Level 1)*
- I can suggest what the lesson of the [Christian] story of ... might be. *(Level 2)*
- I can talk about how a piece of music shows a feeling like happiness or sadness, and why singing together in church is important to Christians. *(Level 2)*

Expectations – Sikhism activities

The following statements are based on the non-statutory QCA expectations for most 9-year-olds in RE, matched to the activities suggested on page 14.

- I can make a link between a piece of Sikh music and a story about Guru Tegh Bahadur which inspired it. *(Level 3)*
- I can suggest answers to questions about why Guru Tegh Bahadur matters to Sikhs, making a link to what matters to me. *(Level 3)*
- I can connect Sikh stories about the Gurus with some of the ideas of the Mool Mantar. *(Level 4)*
- I can ask some questions and suggest some answers from Sikhism about commitment and self-sacrifice, and give my own views on the questions. *(Level 4)*

Using sound to learn about Christianity

For the teacher

Sound is used in a tremendous variety of ways within Christianity. How can pupils be enabled to appreciate something of the capacity of sound to express aspects of belief and faith, worship and commitment, and to reflect on how their own beliefs and ideas might similarly be expressed?

Two strategies for lower primary pupils exemplified through Christianity

Creating sounds and music

→ **Choose a story** with clear Christian teaching that uses images and events which pupils can understand, e.g. a parable or miracle of Jesus (e.g. the good Samaritan or the storm on the lake) or *The Tale of Three Trees* by Angela Hunt (Lion).

→ **Read the story** with the pupils. Talk about where and why Christians might tell the story.

→ **Ask pupils to suggest** how the story could be made easier to understand by adding sound. Make instruments available for pupils to choose from, or ask them to suggest and make the sounds themselves.

→ **Retell the story with children making the appropriate sounds** to illustrate the story. Record it and play it back. What feelings and ideas did they want to show? What choice of instruments did they make and why?

Listening and responding to music

→ **Play a sound or a piece of music** which some Christians might use, in church or at home on their own. Depending on the piece chosen, pupils:

- **listen and respond in movement:** How does the sound or music make them feel? What made them respond in the way they did?

- **listen for a word or sound which is repeated,** e.g. Alleluia, Lord, Amen, a bell. How many times did they hear it? What does it mean? What might this tell us about what Christians believe?

- **retell the story** which the music presents, in words, pictures or drama. What can Christians learn about God from this story?

→ **Watch a clip of Black Pentecostal worship** – focus on the singing, the movements and the facial expressions. Ask children to talk about how they think the worshippers are feeling and what matters to them.

→ **Sing a worship song together** and include some movements a Black gospel choir might use. Perform this in assembly.

Telling a Bible story using sound: The wise and foolish builders (Matthew 7:24–27)

A wise man decided to build himself a new house. He looked around for the best possible place. He found a big flat rock. 'That will do fine!' he thought. He built his house deep into this rock.

The wind blew (*howling wind and whistle sounds*). The rain fell (*rain tube or improvised sounds*). The seas rose (*crashing wave sounds*).

The house didn't move an inch! The man slept safe and snug inside his lovely new home (*zzzzz – sound of man sleeping*).

A foolish man also wanted to build a new house. He found a lovely flat beach – lots of nice sand. 'This will be perfect!' he said to himself. He set about and built a fine house. The sun shone and everything was just wonderful!

But then the wind blew (*howling wind sounds*). The rain fell (*rain tube or improvised sounds*). The seas rose (*crashing wave sounds*).

And guess what? The house fell down! (*crashing sounds*)

Jesus said, 'If you listen to my words and do as I say, you will build your life on something as solid as rock!'

Sing: 'The wise man built his house upon the rock'.

See also...

- ***Religions of the world: voices and instruments in prayer and praise*** by Christine Richards (PCET, 2001). This includes a 77-minute CD-ROM of music and sounds from six world religions, plus Jainism and Shinto. The pack includes notes for use, and a large poster. www.pcet.co.uk

- **Contemporary Christian worship music**: Sticky Music (www.stickymusic.co.uk) produces a wide range of titles, some of which can used in the RE classroom.

- ***Using Music in Religious Education*** by Catherine Mitchell explores ways in which music can be used in RE at Key Stage 2. http://farmington.virtualsite.co.uk

- **Primary National Strategy:** *Listening – making it work in the classroom* (DfES 0624–2003 G). See DfES website for details.

Exploring Sikhism through sound and visual stimulus: ICT activities for RE

For the teacher

Singing shabad kirtan is a fundamental part of Sikh congregational worship. It is the singing of God's praises, usually a musical rendering of the gurbani (hymns found in the Guru Granth Sahib Ji). Kirtan is usually accompanied by tabla (drums) and harmonium.

The internet resource used in this activity for upper primary pupils combines sound with video, which is ideal for the RE classroom where there is a large monitor or interactive whiteboard. Alternative kirtan are readily available on CD-ROM or the internet (see below).

Listening … responding … making links

→ **Show pupils a picture** of Guru Tegh Bahadur (www.srigurugranthsahib.org). Ask them to look closely and to note down details of posture, facial expression, dress, objects, symbols, colours used. What does this suggest about how this person might be regarded by Sikhs? Where might Sikhs place such a picture? What else do pupils need to know before they can give a 'good' answer to these questions?

→ **Play a short extract (sound and video)** of the kirtan about Guru Tegh Bahadur found on www.srigurugranthsahib.org. (Note: start about 60 seconds into the 11–minute clip, where the kirtan itself begins). Ask pupils to focus on the sound and the images shown on the video: What do they notice? What information does the video give about Guru Tegh? Which aspects of the sound and images achieved this? What questions do they now have about Guru Tegh Bahadur?

→ **Provide opportunities for pupils to find out more** about Guru Tegh Bahadur, using textbooks or the internet. What answers can they find to their questions? To think about: What issues might Guru Tegh stand up for today?

→ **Pupils write a letter to the web keeper,** saying what they have learned about Guru Tegh and Sikh beliefs from the website and including a suggestion of something new for the site which they would find helpful.

Guru Tegh Bahadur Sahib Ji

Guru Tegh Bahadur (1621–1675) was the youngest son of Guru Hargobind. He became Guru in 1664 at a time when Sikhs were increasingly being persecuted, and being asked to renounce their faith.

Guru Tegh Bahadur believed that everyone should be free to worship God in whatever way they believed to be right; he led the Sikhs in battle to fight for this right.

He and four of his closest followers refused to renounce their faith. They were captured and imprisoned, and then tortured and killed. Guru Tegh Bahadur is remembered today as a Guru-martyr.

For more detail see
www.sgpc.net/gurus/guruteghbahadur.asp

See also...

Information about kirtan (also *keertan*)
• www.srigurugranthsahib.org/featured/kirtan.htm

Kirtan on CD-ROM
• DTF Asian Books & Musicals, 117 Soho Road, Handsworth, Birmingham, B21 9ST. *Tel:* 0121 515 1183 *Web:* www.dtfbooks.com

Kirtan online (sound files)
• www.gurbani.org/kirtan.htm
• www.siplweb.com/psp/asp/audio.asp
• www.gursikhi.org/keertanpage.htm

Exploring the meaning of visual images

For the teacher

Visual images are powerful. They can excite the eye and trigger the imagination and emotions. It is not surprising that religions have used visual imagery so much throughout the centuries, for images can be used to express belief and can be an important part of worship practices. For others, visual images provide a 'window', through which we may glimpse the beliefs and practices of a religion, often teasing us to find out more.

The activities suggested on the following pages aim to help pupils explore and interpret some visual images found in Islam, Christianity and Hinduism.

As well as a powerful means of learning about religion, these activities can contribute to the creative and mathematical development of pupils; assist in the development of speaking and listening skills; and encourage thinking and reflection skills.

The activities can be adapted for either upper or lower primary pupils.

Things to note

These suggestions complement the QCA schemes of work:

3A What do signs and symbols mean in religion?

3B How do Hindus celebrate Divali?

6B Worship and community: What is the role of the mosque?

6F How do people express their faith through the arts?

Introducing Islamic art

- Visual images in Islam convey order and pattern.
  A basic Muslim belief is that only the existence of Allah can explain the wonders and orderly patterns found in life, in nature, and in time.
  Order and pattern are characteristic of the Muslim life. The infinitely repeating patterns both in artistic design and in patterns of worship represent the unchanging laws of God.

- Within Islam, people do not appear in specifically religious art. Muhammad or any of the other prophets may not be represented in any form. Some Muslim children may not be allowed to draw the human form at all.

- The three major Islamic art forms are:
  - calligraphy – used to write out passages from the Qur'an – books are a major art form;
  - architecture;
  - geometric designs and the interweaving of floral patterns known as arabesque. Many Islamic patterns represent the infinite, repeating themselves for ever.

See also... useful websites: Islamic art

- Downloadable Islamic geometric designs: www.islamicart.com
- Details for creating Islamic patterns: www.thegrid.org.uk/hertsmathsyear2000/mecss/islamic.html
- For an easy-to-work applet which designs Islamic star patterns and is good to use on an electronic whiteboard: www.cgl.uwaterloo.ca/~csk/washington//taprats/
- Gateway site for Islamic art: http://re-xs.ucsm.ac.uk/re/religion/islam/art.html
- Year 2 school activity making Islamic patterns: atschool.eduweb.co.uk/southwold.school/ islampat.htm

Activity cards for pupils: Exploring Islamic patterns

Card 1
Talk about...

Card 2

→ Talk about the pictures on card 1.

→ What do they have in common?

→ Where might you find them?

Card 3
Talk about...

They are all patterns and designs found in mosques.

→ Who uses a mosque?

→ What is a mosque used for?

Card 4
Try this

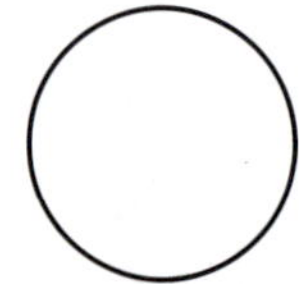

This shape is often found in Islamic art.

→ Put a pencil point anywhere on the circle, and trace round the shape.

→ What do you notice?

→ Is there a beginning or an ending anywhere?

→ What do you think is the 'hidden message' in the shape?

→ What might this 'say' about God for a Muslim?

Card 5
Try this

Your teacher will give you an enlarged copy of a geometric pattern. Colour in one shape on the pattern. (Popular Muslim colours are greens, blues, golds). Now find and colour the same shape in somewhere else in the design.

→ How many times could you repeat this activity?

→ What might this endless repetition of the same shape over and over again within the design tell you about what Muslims believe about God?

→ Design a pattern you think would be pleasing to a Muslim.

For the teacher

Photocopy and cut out the cards. Give them out in sequence, allowing time for pupils to discuss and work through them in pairs.

Notes

• Because circles have no end they are infinite – and so they remind Muslims that Allah is infinite.

• Complex geometric designs create the impression of unending repetition, and this helps a person get an idea of the infinite nature of Allah.

Exploring a Christian image with pupils

For the teacher

Examples of Christian art abound, some dating back to the earliest days of Christianity.

Hunger cloths or Lenten veils

The activity here uses a contemporary example of Christian art. For a number of years, up to the year 2000, a German Roman Catholic organisation called Misereor commissioned artists around the world (usually from developing countries) to create a 'Lenten veil' which would be used as a focus for Christian worship and meditation during Lent.

The example illustrated on the back cover was created for the Millennium by Mr Suryo Indratno, a Javanese artist.

See also…

Hunger cloths can be purchased from a German company – e-mail info@eine-welt-mvg.de

The following websites contain some illustrations:

- www.strath.ac.uk/Departments/SocialStudies/RE/Database/Graphics/Artefacts/jpegs/Christian/hcloth.jpg
- www.stanthonyshrine.org/art_exhibits/Hospitality_art.html

Exploring the Millennium Lenten veil

→ Give pairs of pupils a copy of the Lenten veil (back cover).

→ Pupils look carefully at the image in silence for 2 minutes.

→ Pupils turn the picture face down and, working together, try to sketch or write down all the things they can remember from the image. Allow 5 minutes.

→ **Feedback** – ask pupils:

- What did you draw or write down first? (Is this common to most?)
- Would this have been the artist's intention?
- The picture was designed for the Millennium – 2,000 years since Jesus came. What do you think is the main message in the picture?

→ Turn over the picture and look again. Give each pair a photocopy of the picture on page 18 and one section to focus on. What does it show? What might it mean for a Christian?

→ Everyone feeds back their ideas before each pair is given a copy of the notes on page 18. Pupils compare their own ideas with those in the notes.

Making our own 'Hunger cloth' (creative reflective activity)

→ Give pupils Post-it notes and ask them to write down one hope for the future. In groups of four, pupils share ideas.

→ Give each group a set of 'hope' cards (see below). Pupils add their own 'hope' cards to these. Ask pupils to sort them and agree four most important 'hopes'. Each member takes one 'hope' and, using words, drawings, colours, cut-out pictures and fabric, makes a visual representation of it. Stick the four together to form a group 'Lenten Veil'. Each group presents their work. Others try to work out the hopes from the images.

No more wars	People will share more	People will care more for animals	People will try to do good things for other people
People will listen more to God	Everyone will have a home	People will not be so greedy	People will not be frightened any more
No more bullying	People will not be so cruel to each other	No more poor people	People will care more for each other
People will be kinder to old people and children	Everyone will have enough food	People will care more for the world	No more stealing

The Millennium Lenten veil

The year of the Lord's Favour – a fresh start and liberation for all
By Suryo Indratno, an artist from Java

By following the path outlined below, you can see how the picture has been structured:

1 God the creator, his arms outstretched showing that he still cares for the world and all its people.

2 Country people, who have to work hard, often with little reward for themselves – some are protesting here.

3 A teacher, trying to teach about fairness, justice and peace.

4 Women, including 'mother earth' (lower central figure) representing the injustices to women and children, the rights of the weak and the poor.

5 Victims of terror, including war.

6 The jug being emptied represents the world's natural resources being used up.

7 People from all walks of life, coming together representing 'Christianity'.

8 People have to work really hard to make sure that they do God's will.

9 People from all over the world sit together and share a meal to celebrate peace between them all.

10 The 'Javanese hill tree' challenging all faiths to talk to one another, and for Christians to do their best to avoid conflicts with other faiths.

Interpreting the meaning of some visual images in Hinduism

For the teacher

Hindus make great use of symbolism and colour in their visual images, from the murti statues to pictures of the deities, to the mendhi and rangoli patterns at Divali.

The following activity aims to encourage pupils to look closely at some images of Brahma, Shiva and Vishnu and to identify what the symbols tell us about the character of that god. These three gods are for many Hindus the most important and together they are known as the Trimurti.

Murti is the word for an image or deity used as a focus of Hindu worship. 'Idol' should not be used, and 'statue' may also cause offence.

See also...

A useful website with downloadable murti images is www.strath.ac.uk/Departments/SocialStudies/RE/Database/Graphics/Images/Hindu/Deities.html

Religious Artefacts: Why? What? How? (RE Today Services) has a Shiva murti activity on pages 18–19.

Activities for pupils

Getting started

→ Show pupils a range of everyday objects which 'say' something about you or someone else they know well, e.g. a musical instrument, a favourite book, a map (for someone who likes travel). Tell pupils these are all clues about one person and indicate what that person is like and is interested in. What can they work out from them? Who do they think it is and why?

→ In pairs, pupils could identify the 'symbols' they would pick for each other which tell others something about what they are like.

→ Show pupils a picture of a Hindu god – Shiva is a good one to start with. What clues can they see in the picture? What can they work out from them about the god?

Exploring Hindu murtis:
Worksheet and discussion activity

→ Copy and cut up the lists on page 20, putting packs into separate envelopes – enough for each pair of pupils. Sorting words helps pupils to discuss their thoughts and adjust their conclusions before committing answers to paper.

→ Provide pupils with clear images of one or all of the three murtis. Display on an electronic whiteboard if available.

→ On a blank sheet of paper, pupils draw three columns headed 'Brahma', 'Vishnu' and 'Shiva'. Ask pupils to:

- Look carefully at one of the three murtis with a partner.
- Write down all the things you notice about the image under the correct title on your piece of blank paper.
- Can you identify what the murti is holding?
- Do the same for the other murtis.
- Talk about what the image tells you and make a list of words to describe the kind of god you think he is.
- Look at the contents of the envelope marked 'Trimurti images and objects'. Do any match your observations? Sort the descriptions and match them to the correct murti on your worksheet.
- Open the envelope marked 'Trimurti symbolism'. Sort these statements and match them to the correct item.
- On the worksheet, write down three things you have noticed about each image and what you think each might mean.
- In the last box on your worksheet, create your own murti. This might be a 'Lord of Sport', 'Lady of Good Deeds', 'Lord of Learning' or 'Lady of Courage'. Underneath the image, write three symbols used and write what they mean.

Note: The activity can be simplified by choosing to focus on only one image. Alternatively groups can be given different murtis to explore, followed by a class feedback session.

The Trimurti			My own murti
    Brahma	 Vishnu	 Shiva	 Lord or Lady of...

For the teacher

	Trimurti images and objects	Trimurti symbolism
Brahma	four heads	sees in all directions and knows everything
	riding a swan	wisdom
	book	holy writings
	cup	first living being, came out of water
	beads	prayer
	spoon	offerings made in worship
Vishnu	mace	power of knowledge
	discus	conquering evil
	lotus flower	purity
	conch shell	the first sound of creation – water
	snakes	Hindu creation story
Shiva	demon	ignorance and stupidity
	fire	power
	drum	rhythm of life and creation
	three eyes	seeing the world and what is within
	upheld hand	nothing to fear
	hand pointing down	pointing at the dance of life

Symbols in religion: making meaning

For the teacher: from commercial logos to religious symbols via wedding rings

Symbols are a key to understanding how religious expression works, but it's hard to show small children the depth of meaning involved. In these pages, some active learning ideas about using symbolic images and language are provided.

One way of appreciating the significance of symbols is to look at those which represent charities, such as the wearing of **ribbons** in support of breast cancer charities or those that work with people living with HIV/AIDS.

Pudsey Bear is a symbol of Children in Need, and there are many more – get the children to suggest some, bring them in and look at them together. Talk about how, if someone was to spit at Pudsey, the action would be offensive and far more so than if he was just 'any old teddy bear'. Why? Surely because as a community we have invested some meaning and some sense of caring into the teddy with the eye bandage. So he moves from being a logo to being a symbol.

In the context of human caring, logos can acquire more meaning than their commercial origins suggest, and become symbols of values such as compassion, care, or justice. Just as, in the commonly used symbol of a wedding ring, the band of gold represents the relationship, precious and unbroken, beautiful and imbued with significance. If the ring is lost, then more than money will be mourned. But if the relationship is broken, then gold with a cash value of £200 may become worthless to a person who has worn it for 20 years. The meaning of the relationship has become one with the signifier.

Now think of how the symbols of world religions – the aum, the star and crescent, the cross – have been invested with meaning for centuries by millions. The power of these symbols begins to show.

In this work, we are aiming to show children how powerful symbolic images and words can be. The learning ideas suggested should be fun – but symbols, particularly the religious ones, can have a depth charge that moves and surprises us still.

Things to note

These teaching ideas might be used with reference to a number of QCA Units or Agreed Syllabus Programmes of Study and Scottish RME guidelines.

In particular the work is relevant to QCA units on:

- What are harvest festivals? (Reception)
- How do Jewish people express their beliefs in practice? (1E)
- What do signs and symbols mean in religion? (3A)
- Why are sacred texts important? (6C)

See also...

- *Picturing Jesus* packs A and B (RE Today Services) include some learning ideas and interesting images and symbols from the Christian faith. They are well suited to the needs of visual learners.
- Channel 4 Learning's excellent RE product *Water, Moon, Candle, Tree and Sword* uses a symbols approach and is well suited to the needs of pupils aged 6–8. www.channel4.com/learning

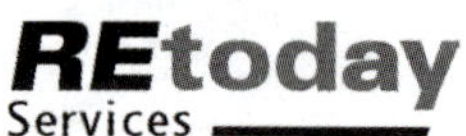

What is the meaning of the bread? Activities for 5–7s

For the teacher

Bread is an important symbol found in religions. For Christians and Jews, bread is a sign of the love of God. Remember how Christians use bread and wine for worship at Holy Communion, and how Jews use bread for worship at home on Shabbat. For children, it is a part of everyday life.

Four useful steps to remember when teaching RE to young children are:

1 **Use an engaging device** – this might be a picture, an object, an artefact – something to grab children's attention.

2 **Exploration** – use strategies to encourage children to ask questions; suggest meanings; talk about and around the 'entering device'.

3 **Set the story, teaching, festival or artefact firmly in the faith context** – how can we tell it is important to believers? What does it mean?

4 **Reflection** – enabling children to look at their own world in light of their learning; to make a link with their own experience.

Bread – thinking about its meaning

→ As an engaging device, the teacher could bring a bread-making machine, make a loaf and taste it in the lesson. The fresh bread smells wonderful! Alternatively, bring in several kinds of fresh bread – French bread, naan, pitta and chapattis – or whatever is available.

→ For exploration, read the story of the Little Red Hen. The themes include hard work, fair shares, laziness, and fruitfulness. Discuss the ideas with the children, and compare the Little Red Hen to the mum in the poem 'Mum's Work'. Ask the children: who can they think of who works so that other people benefit? Is bread a symbol of love? What symbol would they like to choose for their mum, dad or best friend? How would they explain it?

→ Use the diagram on page 23 to talk about the many different types of bread and think about some of the special times when Christians and Jews use bread to show their love for God and for one another.

Mum's work

She cut the wheat
And ground it down
Broke the grains
To find the flour

She took the flour
Poured the water
Pinch of salt
A little yeast

She rolled the mixture
Hand to hand
Kneading dough
As if her life depended on it

She let it rise
She lit the oven
Greased the tin
Shut it in.

She waited long time
Children came home
She served the loaf
Still warm

Small hands broke it
Chewed and laughed
She was content in that minute
Watching her children

They ate the bread she made
They grew strong from her love.

Using the diagram on page 23

Make a blank version of the diagram, with just the bubbles and space for lots of different bread pictures to be stuck on.

Talk together about the 'meaning of bread' idea, stick on pictures of bread and fill in the second circle with meanings children suggest.

Add some of the ideas suggested on page 23. Add a third cirlce of 'thought bubbles' with some sentence starters for pupils to complete.

The meaning of bread

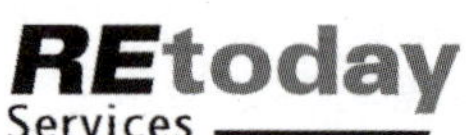

Symbolic words – making metaphors for God with older primary pupils

For the teacher

This strategy focuses on providing pupils with a chance to develop metaphors for God. This is a crucial skill in the area of symbol and religious expression. Here's a simple way to approach the topic which never fails to be interesting, and relates pupils' learning about any particular religion to their own responses effectively. It is a piece of 'real RE' using higher order thinking skills in a 'deep thinking, low writing' structure.

If God was a...

- flower...
- colour...
- plant...
- tree...
- mineral...
- food...
- toy...
- building...
- light...
- animal...
- drink...
- item of clothing...
- character from the movies...

it would be...

because...

Activity for pupils: Theological metaphorical work with 8-year-olds(!)

The following activity is a great way to get 180 theological thoughts out of a class of pupils in about 20 minutes! Try it: you'll be pleased with the results.

→ Put the statements 'If God was a...' up round the walls on large sheets of paper. Give each pupil six sticky Post-it notes to write on.

→ Ask pupils to choose six of the prompts and write their own ideas about God into some metaphors. Use some of the examples given on the following page to stimulate good thinking and clarify the form for the pupils.

→ Get pupils in twos and threes to look at one sheet, and summarise for the rest of the class what the metaphors say about God. They could do this on an OHP slide or interactive whiteboard.

Follow-up discussion

Some probing questions to ask:

- What is God like?
- Why do some people believe, but not others?
- Why is it hard to describe God?
- Where do our ideas about God come from?
- What are the best symbols for God?

Two homework questions

- What did you do in RE today?
- What did you learn from doing this?

(RE too rarely fits in to primary school homework timetables, which are dominated by 'core subjects'.)

Note

These areas of RE connect closely to literacy skills and can be linked to literacy work on figurative, metaphorical and symbolic uses of language in poetry and other text-level work.

Some metaphors from 7–11-year-olds on the topic of God

Most of these are 'God-positive' but there are some from young atheists and agnostics – these are grouped at the end of the list.

If God was a kind of weather it would be **lightning** because God's frightening.

If God was a body part it would be the **heart** because God gives us life and keeps us going.

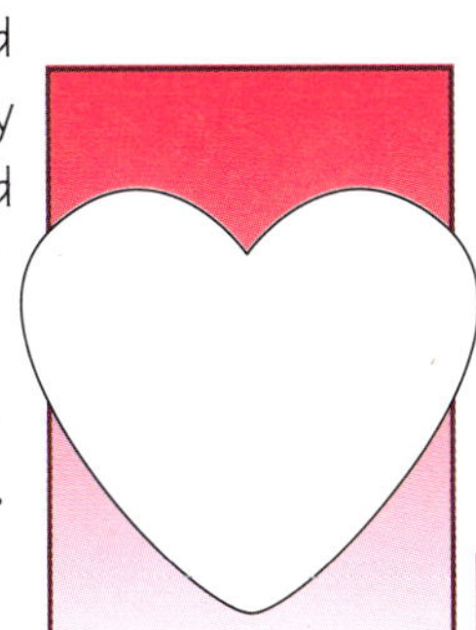

If God was a TV show it would be **Alive and Kicking** because He always is.

If God was a piece of equipment it'd be a **mobile phone** because you can talk any time.

If God was a colour it would be **all colours**, because God is everywhere and everything.

If God was a car it would be a **stretch limo** because He goes on for ever.

If God was a food it would be **vegetables** because he is good for you.

If God was a food it would be **bread** because it keeps you healthy.

If God was a flower it'd be a **poppy**, a reminder of those who died for us, like Jesus.

If God was a flower it would be a **forget-me-not** because God doesn't forget anything.

If God was an item of clothing it would be **armour**, because he keeps you safe.

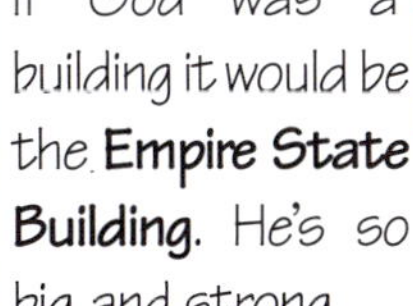

If God was a building it would be the **Empire State Building**. He's so big and strong.

If God was a movie character, it would be **Santa**, because they both don't exist.

If God was a bird it would be a **dodo**, because they're both out of date.

If God was an animal, it would be a **unicorn**. Both are just legends.

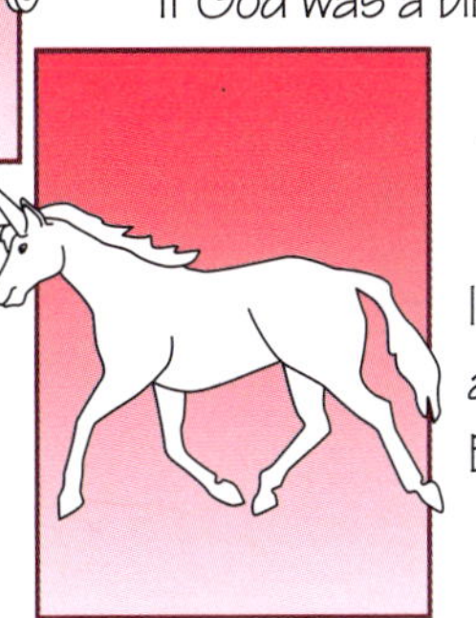

Going further: four extension ideas for higher-achieving pupils

→ In Saint John's gospel, Jesus uses seven symbols to describe himself, including: 'I am the door, the way, the light, the shepherd, the vine.' Ask pupils to suggest: in what ways was Jesus like these symbols?

→ In Jewish scripture, God is likened to a shepherd, a parent, a lover, a king. God is called the Almighty, the Ancient of Days, the Creator, the Most High. Ask pupils: what do these descriptions show about Jewish beliefs?

→ In Islam, there are Ninety-nine Names given to Allah. These include The Judge, The Rich One, The Defender, The Light, The Discoverer, The Nourisher. Taking care to note that Muslims do not compare Allah to mere humans, what do these Names tell us about Muslim understanding of God?

→ What is the same about how Christians, Jews and Muslims speak about God? What is distinctive for each of these religions?

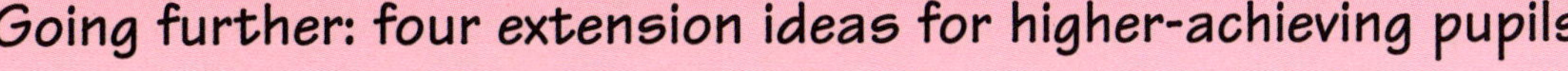

Religious artefacts in the classroom – symbolic expressions of meaning

For the teacher

Religious artefacts can provide teachers and pupils with invaluable 'windows' into faith communities. With careful and sensitive use, pupils can explore their symbolic meaning and reflect on the beliefs and experiences they express for members of a faith community.

Seen in this way, artefacts become vital 'tools' for RE. Through these special objects, the 'essence' of belief and practice can be explored, interpreted and reflected upon.

They are much more than just interesting display objects for the classroom or entrance hall.

Sensitivities about using artefacts – some tips

Teachers are often concerned about the sensitive use of religious artefacts in the classroom. Some good tips are:

→ Be careful about allowing children to dress up in an artefact or religious symbol not 'their own'. For example it may not be appropriate to ask a Jewish child to put on a crucifix or a Muslim to wear a tallit. If possible always consult with parents or members of local faith communities.

→ Store and handle religious artefacts in a similar way to how a faith community member would. For example when handling a Qur'an wash hands and cover head before touching, and store on a high shelf. Teachers need to encourage and enable pupils to show respect to other people's religious sensibilities, and this modelling behaviour is one way in which this can be done.

Prayer artefacts from four world faiths

A practical note: organisation and storage

Clearly mark and store according to religion (in storage boxes, trays in a cabinet or even old suitcases).

Make sure each item is clearly identifiable. Use a digital camera to photograph and label each artefact, e.g. kippah – cap – Judaism; kirpan – sword – Sikhism. The time invested will prolong the usefulness of your artefact collection.

Organise your collection systematically according to religion. This minimises the chance of confusing artefacts from one faith with those of another and avoids the possibility of giving offence by keeping artefacts from different faiths together.

Teachers will still be able to select items from each faith collection for use during a particular theme. For example, an exploration of prayer practices in different religions may bring together a votive candle and rosary from Christianity, a prayer wheel from Buddhism and a prayer mat from Islam.

Encouraging respect – a guided visualisation activity

A key attitude that Religious Education aims to develop is that of respect for the religious beliefs and practices of others.

The use of religiously sensitive artefacts in the classroom is an important means of modelling and practising respect.

- The guided visualisation outlined on page 28 focuses attention on something of personal significance in a vulnerable situation.
- It aims to help pupils empathise with the feelings of faith community members about the objects that are special to them.
- In follow-up discussion, encourage pupils to recognise the privilege of handling special religious artefacts in the classroom and how important it is to treat them with the same respect we would want others to show to our special things.

For the teacher: Guided visualisation as a teaching strategy

- Given appropriate preparation, pupils enjoy this activity because it enables them to use their imaginations to get inside stories and experiences.
- It is essentially a 'right brain' activity in which all the senses can play a part; pupils can touch, taste, see, hear and even smell with their imaginations!
- Plan follow-up activities to enable pupils to express their responses verbally, in writing (e.g. poetry) or artistically.

For further information see:

- *A to Z Practical Learning Activities* by Joyce Mackley and Pamela Draycott (RE Today Services)
- *Reflections*, edited by Rosemary Rivett (RE Today Services)
- *Don't just do something, sit there* by Mary Stone (RMEP, ISBN 1-85175-105-X)

Using artefacts to consolidate and extend learning

With careful planning the same artefact can be used on a number of occasions, but make sure that the activities become progressively more challenging as children get older.

For example: A Seder plate

6-year-olds might draw and label a Seder plate, identifying the special foods and making links to the story of Moses and the Passover.

10-year-olds might explore the feelings and experiences the symbolic foods express and begin to make connections with their own feelings of joy, sadness and anticipation of new beginnings.

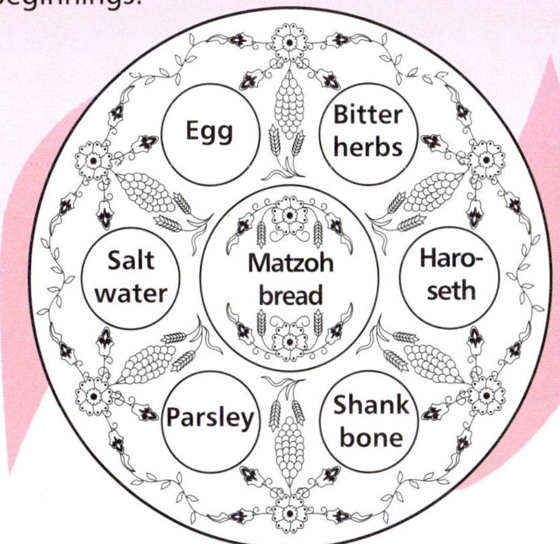

See also...

Suppliers of artefacts

Articles of Faith, Resource House, Kay Street, Bury BL9 6BU
0161 763 6232
www.articlesoffaith.co.uk

Religion in Evidence, Unit 7 Monk Road, Alfreton, Derbyshire DE55 7RL
01773 830255
wwww.tts-shopping.com

Both providers stock a wide range of religious artefacts and both also have publications that help teachers in using them.

My special object: A guided visualisation script

Aim

To help focus attention on the importance and significance of religious artefacts for believers.

Preparation

Ask pupils to sit quietly in a circle with their feet firmly on the floor and hands resting on their lap.

Explain that you are going to lead them on a 'journey' in their imagination and that during the 'story' you will ask some questions and help them to think about their feelings. Explain that they are not expected to answer out loud, but just to think about these quietly.

Encourage them all to take part, but let them know that they can opt out – if anyone does they must not disturb the others, but simply sit quietly until the activity ends.

Read slowly and deliberately, allowing 'space' and 'silence'.

I want you to close your eyes (if you wish) and breathe normally … notice your breath as it enters and leaves your body. *(Pause)*

Now I want you to picture in your mind one object or possession that is very important to you – it may be something someone special has given you, it may be something that you have made, it may be worth a lot of money or very little … Picture it in your mind now … Think about what it looks like. *(Pause)*

Now picture yourself holding it … what does it feel like … Is it heavy or light? … What colours do you see? … Think about why it is important to you … What does it mean to you? How does it make you feel? *(Pause)*

Now I want you to picture yourself and your special thing with another person nearby. This person is someone you don't know very well; you don't know if you can trust them; you don't know if they are nice or nasty … Picture yourself, your special thing and that person all together right now … The other person is reaching out towards your special object … what do you want to do? Why do you want to do this? *(Pause)*

Now in your imagination I want you to give your special thing to that other person … give it to them and see them taking it … How does this make you feel? … Now see the person looking at your special thing, holding it, touching it … Notice how they are handling it … Are they being careful or rough? Now see them give it back to you safe and sound … How do you feel now? *(Pause)*

You now have your special thing back with you – touch it, feel it, smell it … Now let it go back to the place where you keep it … safe and secure. *(Pause)*

Still breathing slowly and deeply, I want you to begin to take notice of the things around you in this room. When you are ready, open your eyes, look around you but remain silent.

Follow-up

Without talking, go to your table and sit down. You will find a piece of paper with a circle drawn on it.

→ In the circle, draw a picture of your special object.

→ To one side, write some words to show what this object means to you and why it is special.

→ On the other side, write some words to describe how you felt when a stranger was handling your special object.

Preparation for class discussion

What advice would you give someone about handling objects of special value and meaning? Write down some ideas.

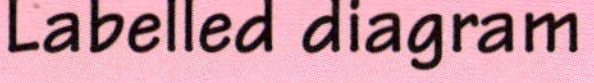

Some classroom strategies using artefacts

Hide and describe

Place the artefact inside a feely bag or mystery box. Pupils take turns to feel and describe the hidden artefact.

Useful for: involving all pupils; encouraging observation through touch; developing interpretation (ask children – What do you think it is? How do you know?); developing speaking and listening skills.

For example: in a unit on Hanukkah in Judaism, place a menorah (seven-branched candlestick) in one bag and a hanukiah (eight-branched with feeder candle) in another. Pupils respond to questions such as: What are they? How are they similar or different? What do you think they are used for?

Labelled diagram

Pupils label and explain features of an artefact.

Useful for: encouraging careful observation and interpretation; structuring research and recording.

For example: Give pupils a diagram of a Hindu murti such as Shiva or Krishna. Ask them to suggest what each feature means, for example: How many arms has Shiva got? What do you think this means?

Questioning

Useful for: introducing a religious artefact for the first time.

Ask pupils to:

→ work out three questions they would ask the maker, user, owner or seller of the artefact;

→ respond to some simple questions to encourage close observation and reflection, for example: What is it made of? What do you notice most about it? What do you think it is? Who do you think might use this?

For example: introducing Sikhism through pictures of the Gurus along with a khanda and a representation of the Ik Onkar.

Using a religious artefact as a stimulus for personal reflection

Look at how a religious artefact is used within the religion and adapt the idea to help pupils reflect on some aspect of their own life.

For example: A classroom mezuzah

After studying the use of the mezuzah within Judaism, pupils could design and make a classroom or personal 'belief box'.

The mezuzah contains the key beliefs of the Jews. These are fastened to doorposts of Orthodox homes as a reminder of their promises to God as they enter and leave.

Pupils could make a mezuzah containing the classroom rules to be fastened to the door, or a personal values or promises box to be fastened to their bedroom door at home.

Designing a logo or symbol for today

→ Look at some logos and symbols used today.

→ Ask pupils to identify some symbols and say what they mean or make them think about. For example: Pudsey Bear (Children in Need); a sports logo such as Nike; the school badge.

→ Look at some symbols for different religions. Consider what shapes and colours are good to represent any religions they have studied.

→ Ask them to design a new 'logo' for Christianity or another religion for today. See PCfRE's Spirited Arts gallery (www.pcfre.org.uk/spiritedarts) for pupils' ideas for a logo for RE.

Bracelets – an approach to artefacts for young children

For the teacher

Exploring and making bracelets is a good way of helping younger children to begin to learn how objects can be used to show what we feel about others and what we think is important.

The following activities make links with the children's own experiences and contribute towards the early learning goals, particularly those to do with developing understanding and respect for others' cultures and beliefs, as well as helping communication and creative development.

Activities for younger pupils

→ Show children a bracelet – it may be a special one of your own or perhaps one given to a baby at baptism. Talk about how we often give bracelets to show love or friendship.

→ Make a simple 'friendship bracelet'. Talk about who they would give it to and why.

→ If possible show children some special 'religious' bracelets. Look at a rakhi and hear about how it is used in the Hindu festival of Raksha Bandhan to show love between brothers and sisters. Children could act out ways they can show they love their brothers and sisters. (Note: friendship bracelets of today have their origins in this Hindu tradition.)

→ Introduce a WWJD bracelet (available from many Christian bookshops). What do children think it is? Ask pupils to look very carefully at it. What do they notice? What might the letters mean? Who do they think might wear it? Make up an everyday situation in which a Christian child might be helped by thinking about WWJD.

→ Look carefully at a kara. Look at a video clip or poster of someone wearing one. Explain that it is very special and that the shape tells us something about what a Sikh person thinks is really important. Feel its weight, its strength, its shape. Ask children to suggest words to describe it. Talk, draw and write about what children wear to show who or what they belong to, e.g. their school uniform.

A Christian bracelet

WWJD was created in 1989 when Christians in a church in Michigan, USA decided that they always wanted to remind themselves of what Jesus would do in their everyday lives. To remind them to do this they created a simple bracelet – on it were the letters WWJD? Today it is not just bracelets but mugs, T-shirts, caps and even teddy bears!

What Would Jesus Do?

A Sikh bracelet

Many Sikh children, and all adult Sikhs who belong to the Khalsa (Sikh community), wear a kara. This steel band symbolises the eternal nature of God. It is one of the Five Ks – the outward symbols worn to show others that they are Sikh and proud of it.

A bracelet from Hinduism

Raksha Bandhan day symbolises love, affection and a feeling of brotherhood. Sisters tie a piece of thread, called rakhi, around the wrists of their brothers, praying for their long life and happiness.

'On this Raksha Bandhan Day
I send you a Rakhi and firmly pray:
May the glowing Rakhi,
Which adorns your wrist today,
Light your heart with joy and hope
And with love that's strong and true
May it brighten all your days,
Bringing health and
strength to you.
God bless you, my
dear brother.'
Verse from a
greetings card

A painted cross – an activity to help older primary pupils express their learning using art and symbol

For the teacher

- The cross is a universal symbol for Christians, expressing belief, commitment and devotion to Jesus, whom they believe to be the son of God, who died on a cross and rose to life again.

- It is found in numerous forms. The painted crosses of Latin America are just one twentieth century form. They depict in vibrant primary colours the inspirational stories of Christians who fought for social justice and liberation from oppression.

See also...

- Painted crosses can be viewed at www.strath.ac.uk/ Departments/SocialStudies/ RE/Database

- *The Christ We Share* pack (CMS and USPG, 1999)

- A-cross the world (CMS) – www.cms-uk.org

- Pictures or replicas of this type of cross can be purchased from religious artefacts suppliers or from many Christian bookshops.

An activity for older primary pupils

Context: Pupils have been studying the life of a famous Christian – perhaps Martin Luther King or Mother Teresa.

Useful for...

- drawing together learning at the end of a unit on commitment or special people;

- enabling pupils to demonstrate their knowledge and understanding of the individual, and their ability to reflect on and express their ideas about why the cross is an appropriate symbol for them.

It is a good summative assessment activity.

Process

→ Show pupils a painted cross – ideally a real one but, if not, display a picture using an OHT or an image from a website. The Maria Gomez cross is a good one for children. She was a young mother and teacher who died because of her Christian principles. (See below for resource details.)

→ Notice together how the cross illustrates key aspects of the person's life – how it gives us a 'picture' of her. Talk about why it is in the form of a cross – why is this symbol appropriate? (The cross reminds Christians of how Jesus died for others, but also how he came back to life and lives on in spirit to inspire others to live as he did.)

→ Ask pupils: If you were the artist asked to make a painted cross for Martin Luther King or Mother Teresa, what key aspects of his or her life would you choose to show and why? In pairs pupils work out some answers, roughly sketch out their own designs and feed back to the class.

→ Individually, in pairs or in groups, pupils make a painted cross. Use primary colours. Groups could each be given one aspect, the pieces being assembled to make a large wall cross.

→ Follow with an individual reflective activity using sentence starters such as: 'If I could be like MLK in one way it would be...'; 'MLK believed that... What I think about this is...'; 'If MLK came to this school or country today he would...'
These are then added to the wall display.

Symbols in six religious traditions

Card game activities

Enlarge and copy these symbols to make enough packs for your pupils to have one between two.

The following sorting and matching games are based on the traditional children's favourites – Snap and Concentration. Perhaps your pupils will be able to suggest others.

The activities encourage recognition and interpretation of symbolic artefacts and actions, and support speaking and listening skills.

Note: Make sure pupils understand that they are not allowed to keep the matched pair unless the explanation they give satisfies their partner.

Snap

In pairs, children take it in turns to place a card face up. When two cards from the same religion follow on, the first person to shout 'snap' correctly collects the pair. Pupils have to explain the connection between the cards before they can take them. The pupil with the most pairs wins.

Concentration

As above, but this time all the cards are placed face down and pupils take it in turns to turn over two cards. If they are from the same religion and the pupil+ can explain the connection the player keeps the pair. The player with most pairs wins.